CAD $7.99/USD $5.95

I0806884

Kevin Locke

The Seventh Direction: A Legend of Creation Lesson Plan

March 19th, 2024

ISBN - 978-1-77854-032-5

Welcome

Welcome to The Seventh Direction: A Legend of Creation lesson plans. We have included multiple lesson plans for you to use including comprehension questions, crosswords, a word search, colouring pages, and other activities that will help to facilitate engagement with the teachings within the book.

The author, Kevin Locke, passed away unexpectedly before he could approve these lesson plans. However, these lesson plans have been created with Indigenous educators to ensure authenticity and respect for Kevin's work and legacy.

Medicine Wheel Publishing acknowledges that this lesson plan was created on the unceded traditional territory of the Coast Salish People including the Sc'ianew people, the Lekwungen people and the T'Sou-ke people.

Contents

Introduction: Before Reading Activities

Take some time to discuss the title of the book with your class.

- What might the story be about, based on the title, The Seventh Direction: A Legend of Creation?
- What directions can you think of from the top of your head?
- What might the fifth, sixth and seventh directions be?
- What is a creation legend? Can you think of any that you already know of?

Once you have finished discussing, take some time to look at the illustrations on the cover for any hints as to what the book may be about.

- What is included on the cover?
- Is there anything important about the woman on the front of the cover? Where is she holding her hands?
- How many animals can you spot on the cover?

With your class, read the blurb on the back of the book. Brainstorm any keywords you notice from this section. See if you can work together to note down anything students may be confused about, or questions to return to once you have finished reading the book.

Read both the author and illustrator bios at the end of the book. You could have the class do some research and learn more about the lives of Kevin and Kristy, to help understand the spirit and intention that has gone into this book. You could also locate, on a map of Turtle Island, the traditional territories where both creators are from.

Activity 1: Comprehension Questions

Read the story with your class. Once you have finished the story, make sure to read the Glossary of 'Lakota Language Words' at the end of the book to familiarize your class with using these words. Students could even try to use Lakota words in sentences to help consolidate their learning.

Have students answer some questions about the story. If they need to, they are welcome to refer to the book for help.

- Who is Wakȟáŋ Tȟáŋka?
- What happened on the first four days of the creation of the world?
- What are the fifth and sixth directions?
- Explain Wakȟáŋ Tȟáŋka's reasoning as to why the human spirit had to be hidden in such a special place.
- List all the animals that offered Wakȟáŋ Tȟáŋka suggestions on where to hide the human spirit.
- What do you think it means when Wakȟáŋ Tȟáŋka refers to the two-legged? What do you think it means to refer to the four-legged?
- How did Wakȟáŋ Tȟáŋka respond to Tȟatȟáŋka? Why was that?
- Why did Matȟó suggest to hide the human spirit in the deepest cave within the mountains?
- What was Wahíŋheya's suggestion to Wakȟáŋ Tȟáŋka? Why do you think Wakȟáŋ Tȟáŋka chose this suggestion?
- Describe the most memorable part of the book for you. Why was it meaningful to you?
- How long did it take Wakȟáŋ Tȟáŋka and the animals to decide on where to hide the human spirit?
- Why do you think that every animal's suggestion for a hiding place was so unique?
- Why is the human spirit so sacred?
- List some examples from the book which show the connection and unity between everything within this world.

Activity 1: Comprehension Questions (continued)

Guide a discussion with your class on some of the important teachings within this story. You could incorporate the following:

- Why do you think the author, Kevin Locke, said, “We must do our best to be a good relative, not just to the two-leggeds, but to all of creation”? Consider the role the animals had in helping Wakȟáŋ Tȟáŋka, and how the creation of the human spirit was deeply interconnected to the creation of the entire world. Think of some reasons in your own life as to why this is true, too.
- Why is it important to learn about diverse worldviews on creation legends, particularly an Indigenous worldview? What can we learn by being more inclusive?
- Did this legend help you to see anything in a new light? What are some valuable teachings that you have learned from this creation legend?
- When you think about the human spirit, what does it mean to you? Do you have any memories or experiences that remind you of what it means to hold the human spirit in your heart?

Activity 2: Sentence Jumble

The sentences below are from The Seventh Direction; however, they are all jumbled up! Carefully cut out the sentences, and organise them so that they are in their correct order. When you feel sure of the order, glue them into the boxes below.

But Wakȟáŋ Tȟáŋka shook his head and said, "No, no. These mountains, in time, will be filled with many people. They'll dig many holes and everything they see as valuable will be removed — there will be no hidden places. They'll find it right away."

The intersection of everything in this universe, this creation, is within each one of us. We have the responsibility to guard this precious gift as it does not belong to us but to Wakȟáŋ Tȟáŋka.

With all of the animals moving around the Earth, at that precise moment, Wakȟáŋ Tȟáŋka realized it was now time to make the most precious and most sacred entity in the world — the human spirit.

That's when a little Wahíŋheya (Mole) popped up from underground. He held himself up in the last glimmers of light.

All of the animals sensed an opportunity to offer a contribution. They all rushed forward, competing with each other to be the first to offer that perfect hiding place.

Long ago, the world was created in seven days. Each day, Wakȟáŋ Tȟáŋka (The Great Spirit) began to create all of the mountains, trees, plants, animals, waters, and winds.

Tȟatȟáŋka (The Buffalo) said, "These vast prairies are my domain. I have the speed and the endurance to cross over them, and I can withstand bad weather. I shall take this precious human spirit and hide it."

Activity 3: How can I be a Good Relative?

The importance of relationships and our interconnectedness to all things on Mother Earth is an important teaching.

On page 37 in The Seventh Direction, Kevin Locke says, "We must do our best to be a good relative, not just to the two-leggeds, but to all of creation."

As a class, brainstorm possible actions students could take to show that they are being a good relative to the two-leggeds and all of creation.

Select several actions for further exploration. As a class, plan all the details, challenges, or barriers that have to be thought of in order for their goals to be met.

Have students create a visual representation to demonstrate their ideas. Students should include a figure of themselves along with words describing what they do, or would like to do, to be a good relative. The figure they create could be a drawing or a silhouette. See the following example of how this could look.

Activity Sample

Help my neighbour
Clean up the school yard
Volunteer at the animal shelter
Collect food for the food bank

Activity 4: My Best Hiding Place

This activity will give students an opportunity to creatively draw and think about secret hiding places within nature, and how some of our animal relatives may relate to Mother Earth.

Lead a discussion about some of the animals in the book whose ideas were not mentioned in the story. Have students point out any other animals they can find in the book, then choose one of these animals as an example. What might, for example, the owl choose as the best hiding place for the human spirit? What would be some important things that the owl, in particular, would think about when choosing a location?

Following this discussion, have students choose their own animal from the story. Then, using a graphic organizer, students can plan where that animal might choose to hide the human spirit.

Use any kind of graphic organizer that gives students room to draw and print. An example has been provided on the next page.

After all their artwork and writing is complete, ask students to share about their animal and the special place that they chose!

My Best Hiding Place

Write down the animal that you have selected. Then, in the box below, draw the hiding spot you think that animal would choose. Using the speech bubbles around the box, describe in detail about why you think that they would select that place.

My animal: ____________________

Activity 5: Triangular Storyboard Responses

For this activity, students will respond to various prompts based on the book, The Seventh Direction. Students will develop their perspectives on one of the scenarios below through a written task, then create a storyboard to visually express their ideas.

Below are some prompts teachers could use. Brainstorm responses to these prompts with the class, before having students write their own responses, using the templates provided on pages 13, 14, and 15.

- How can I be a good relative; not just to the two-legged, but to all of creation?
- Wakȟáŋ Tȟáŋka made all things on Mother Earth. What was your best creation? Why was it so important to you?
- How should we respond when our idea is not accepted by someone else? Were Buffalo's and Bear's responses appropriate?

Following this, have students create their own storyboards, using the Triangular Story Set template provided on page 12. Carefully cut along the dotted lines and fold along the solid lines. Students can draw directly onto the storyboard, or glue pieces on. Assemble the storyboard once the drawing is complete.

Students can choose cut outs from the selection of examples provided on page 11 for their responses to the prompts. For instance, if the third prompt is chosen, the storyboard would be made using either Buffalo or Bear as the central figure. Or, if they prefer, have students create their own background. See some samples of storyboards on the next page.

Storyboard Samples

Wakȟáŋ Tȟáŋka made all things on Mother Earth. What was your best creation?

Being a good relative. What can you do to be a good relative?

Storyboard Background Cutout Ideas

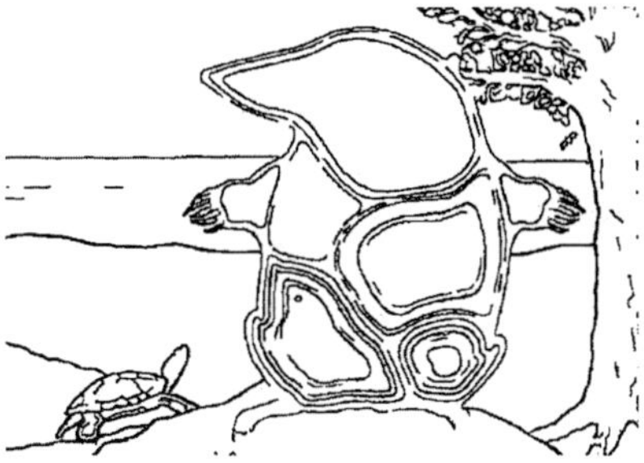

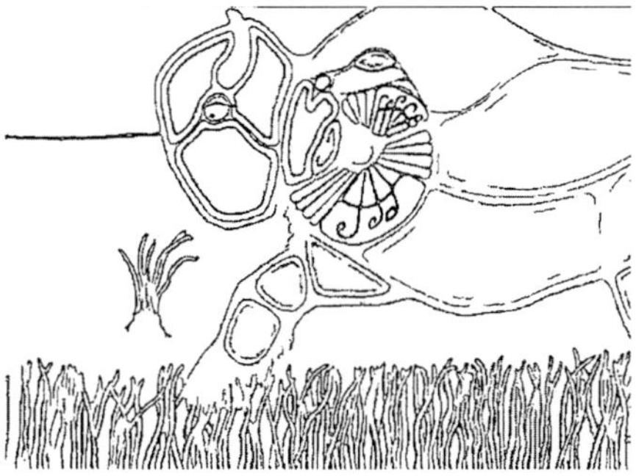

Triangular Story Set

Copy to cardstock.

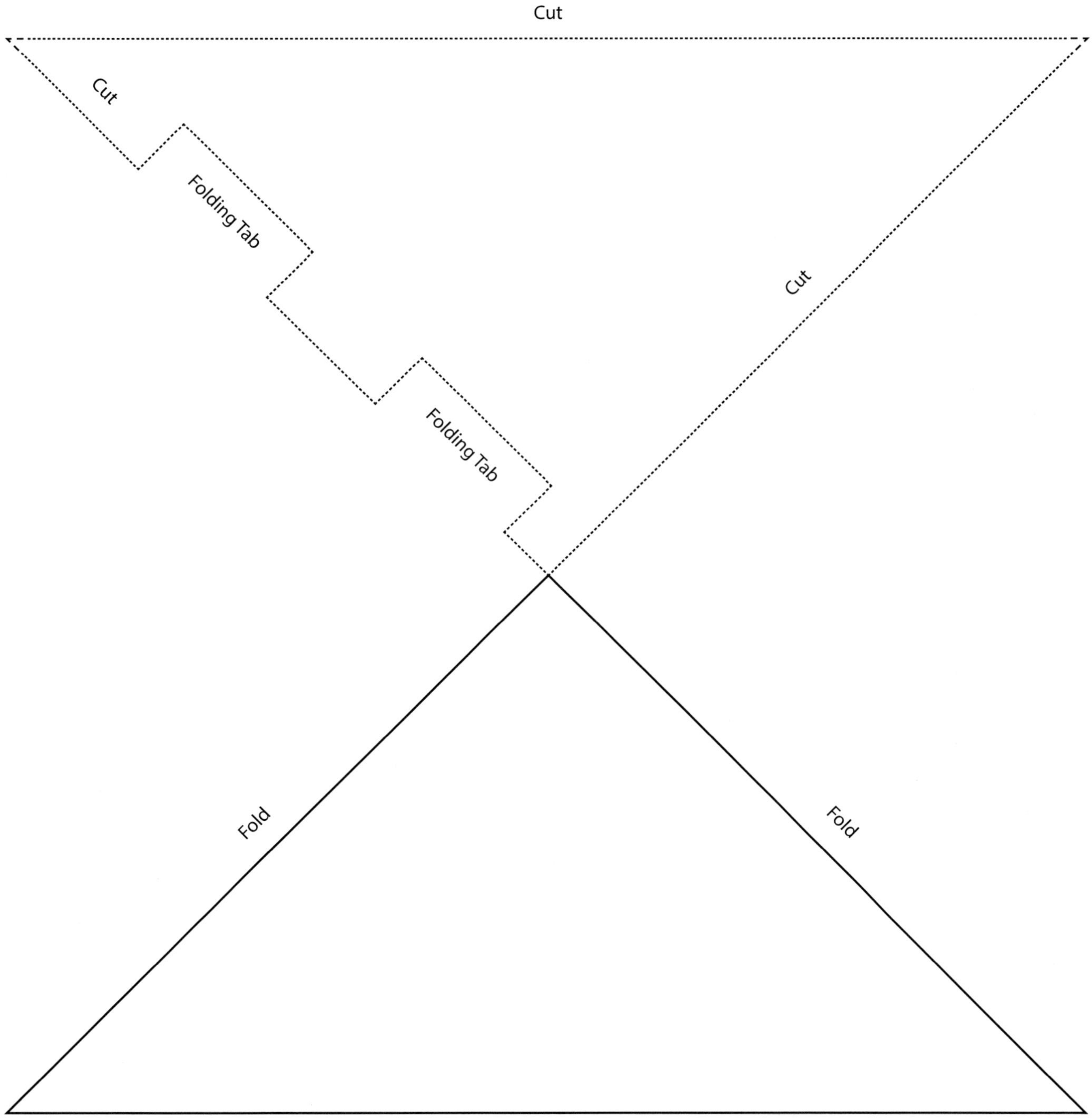

Prompt 1: How can I be a good relative?

You have had a discussion on things you can do to be a "good relative." Write a paragraph on actions you can take to see your plan to completion.

Prompt 2: My very best creation

Wakȟáŋ Thȟáŋka took seven days to make seven great creations! Write a paragraph to share about one of your greatest creations!

Prompt 3: How to respond when my ideas are not acted on

You have had a discussion on how to respond when ideas are shared, but maybe not used. Write a paragraph on a good way to respond when your ideas might not be used.

Activity 6: Word Search

Find the following words in the puzzle. Words are hidden horizontally and vertically.

U	P	E	Y	P	S	P	F	J	C	Q	L	M	J	J	Z	H	S
H	T	H	E	G	R	E	A	T	S	P	I	R	I	T	S	R	N
B	G	R	A	N	D	F	A	T	H	E	R	S	K	Y	G	H	S
E	S	W	Y	N	X	E	B	A	O	K	X	D	O	B	U	Y	V
A	E	L	F	X	P	Z	P	M	O	L	E	S	Q	F	I	W	O
R	V	S	M	F	O	D	I	R	E	C	T	I	O	N	S	K	B
L	E	K	Z	R	I	X	Z	H	U	Z	L	E	G	E	N	D	L
D	N	M	O	U	N	T	A	I	N	O	E	N	L	X	G	O	U
L	G	R	A	N	D	M	O	T	H	E	R	E	A	R	T	H	I
W	Z	Z	B	I	R	D	S	U	Q	X	A	F	W	Z	N	U	T
U	Y	O	B	U	F	F	A	L	O	X	O	H	E	A	R	T	G
K	K	M	T	F	G	C	F	A	P	J	R	T	X	O	V	H	A

Grandmother Earth
The Great Spirit
Grandfather Sky
Directions
Mountain
Buffalo
Legend
Seven
Birds
Heart
Bear
Mole

Activity 7: Lakota Language Crossword

Use the Lakota language words from the book to fill in the answers. Important: remember to use proper accents!

Across

1. My direction begins with an 'N' in English
4. The direction the sun sets in
7. Where all the directions are in motion
8. We walk on her with great respect
9. I was going to hide the gift in a cave

Down

1. The direction the sun comes up
2. Found at the centre of all of us
3. The Seventh Direction that was hidden in the human heart
4. The one who created the Seven Directions
5. My direction starts with an 'S' in English
6. The one who said, "I have instinct"

The Great Spirit - Wakȟáŋ Tȟáŋka

Bear - Matȟó

East - Wiyóhiŋyaŋpata

Mole - Wahíŋheya

South - Itókataǧa

Buffalo - Tȟatȟáŋka

West - Wiyóȟpeyata

The Human Spirit - Taku Wakȟáŋ

North - Wazíyata

Grandfather Sky - Tȟuŋkášila Maȟpíya

Heart - Čhaŋté

Grandmother Earth - Uŋčí Makȟá

Lakota Language Crossword Answers

Across

1. My direction begins with an 'N' in English **(Wazíyata)**
4. The direction the sun sets in **(Wiyóȟpeyata)**
7. Where all the directions are in motion **(Tȟuŋkášila Maȟpíya)**
8. We walk on her with great respect **(Uŋčí Makȟá)**
9. I was going to hide the gift in a cave **(Matȟó)**

Down

1. The direction the sun comes up **(Wiyóhiŋyaŋpata)**
2. Found at the centre of all of us **(Čhaŋté)**
3. The Seventh Direction that was hidden in the human heart **(Taku Wakȟáŋ)**
4. The one who created the Seven Directions **(Wakȟáŋ Tȟáŋka)**
5. My direction starts with an 'S' in English **(Itókataǧa)**
6. The one who said, "I have instinct" **(Wahíŋheya)**

The Great Spirit - Wakȟáŋ Tȟáŋka

Bear - Matȟó

East - Wiyóhiŋyaŋpata

Mole - Wahíŋheya

South - Itókataǧa

Buffalo - Tȟatȟáŋka

West - Wiyóȟpeyata

The Human Spirit - Taku Wakȟáŋ

North - Wazíyata

Grandfather Sky - Tȟuŋkášila Maȟpíya

Heart - Čhaŋté

Grandmother Earth - Uŋčí Makȟá

Activity 8: English Language Crossword

Use the clues to fill in the words. Words can go across or down. Letters are shared when words intersect.

cross

A direction that begins with an 'S'
The one who made the Seven Directions
This direction begins with the letter 'N'
This animal wanted to hide the Seventh Direction
t on the prairies
. We are to walk on her with great respect
. The direction the sun comes up

Down

1. This animal became upset when his idea wasn't used by the Great Spirit
3. At the centre of each human where the human spirit was placed
4. Where all the ancestors were put into motion
5. The most sacred direction created by the Great Spirit
9. Where the sun sets each evening
11. This animal had the best idea for a hiding place

English Language Crossword Answers

Across

. A direction that begins with an 'S' **(south)**
. The one who made the Seven Directions **the great spirit)**
. This direction begins with the letter 'N' **(north)**
. This animal wanted to hide the Seventh Direction ut on the prairies **(buffalo)**
0. We are to walk on her with great respect **grandmother earth)**
2. The direction the sun comes up **(east)**

Down

1. This animal became upset when his idea wasn't used by the Great Spirit **(bear)**
3. At the centre of each human where the human spirit was placed **(heart)**
4. Where all the ancestors were put into motion **(grandfather sky)**
5. The most sacred direction created by the Great Spirit **(the human spirit)**
9. Where the sun sets each evening **(west)**
11. This animal had the best idea for a hiding place **(mole)**

Activity 9: How to make cardstock Matȟó

se this activity so students can get creative and make a cardstock Matȟó (bear). First, make a copy of the template on the following page for each student. Have a wide variety of coloured cardstock ready.

n the template, you will see that there are a variety of different shapes. These are all ifferent parts of Matȟó! Much like a puzzle, students will use these shapes to recreate their very own Matȟó.

lave students carefully cut out all the different shapes below. Students will tape these hapes to coloured cardstock. Use as many colours as you would like for the different pieces. Be creative!

Once everything has been secured, students will carefully cut around the shapes on the cardstock that they have chosen.

n a background of their choosing (this could be another colour of cardstock, or even landscape that they have drawn themselves) arrange all the pieces of Matȟó togeth-r. Once the pieces are test-fitted into position, carefully glue them into place. Be sure pieces are in their proper places! Students can check by looking through the book.

Now Matȟó is all finished! Place heavy books on top of the art project as the glue finishes drying. It helps the project come out nice and flat!

Activity 9: How to make cardstock Matȟó

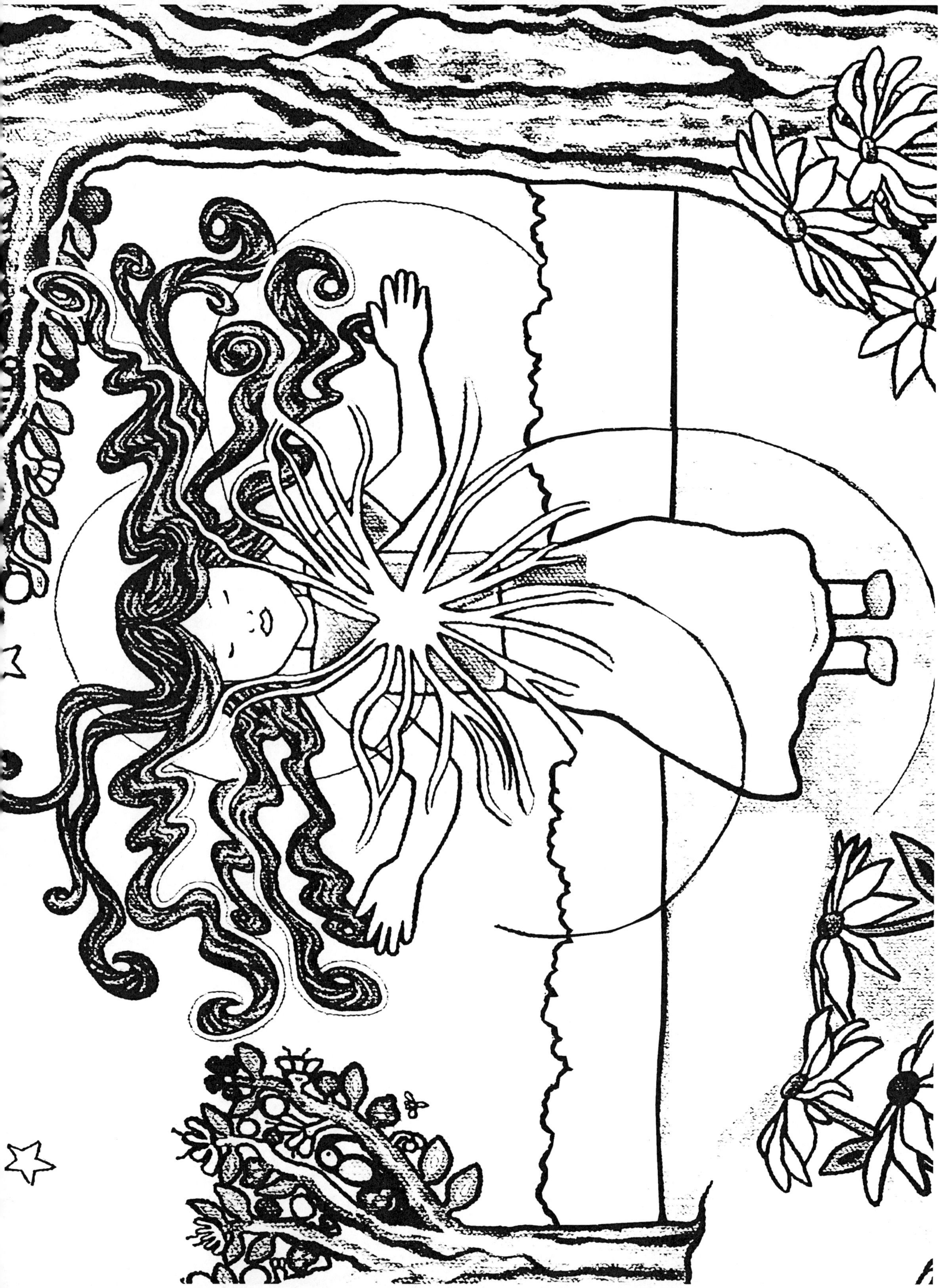

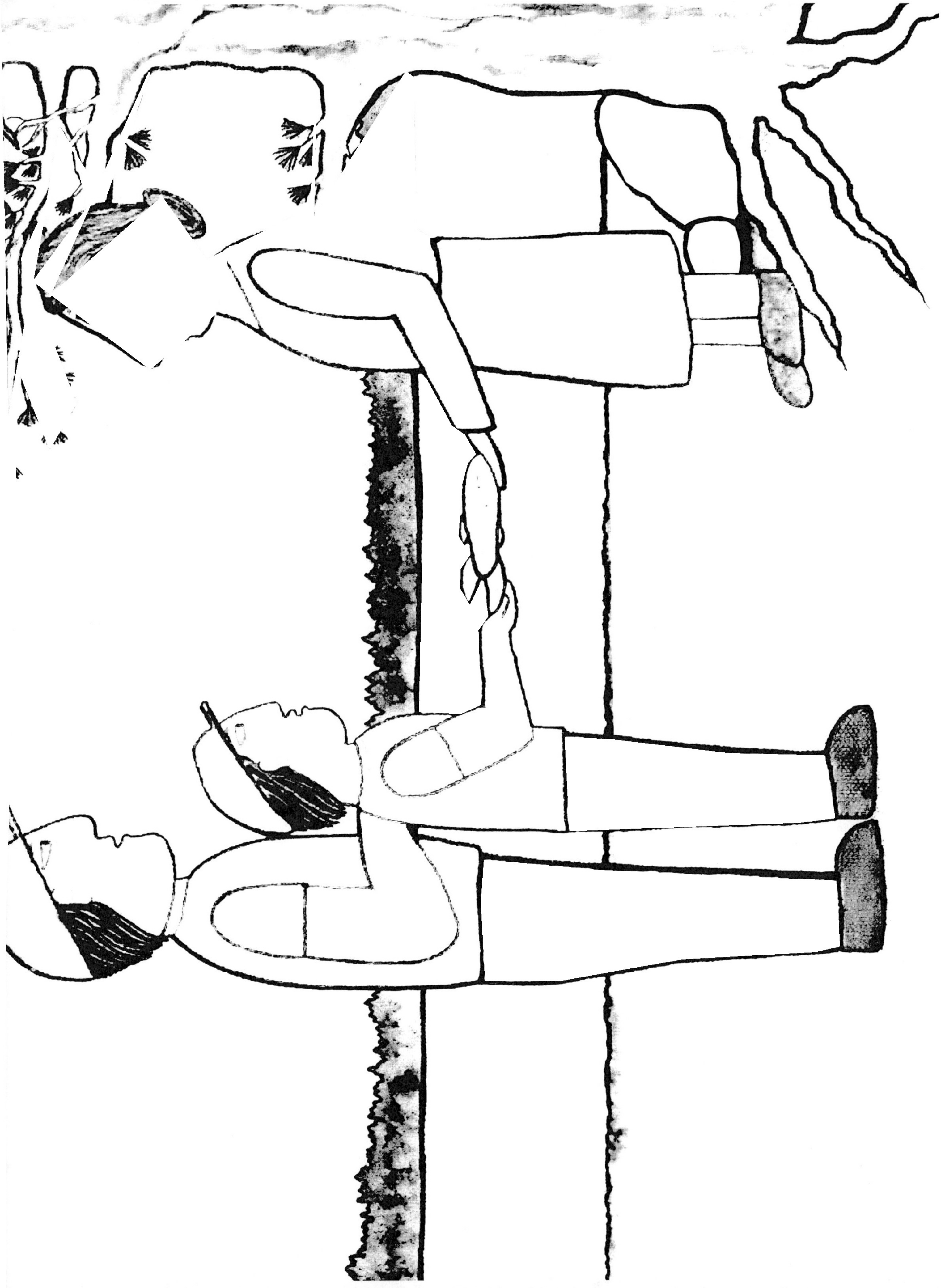